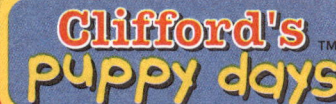

MW01610839

THE LITTLE RED SLED

By Tisha Hamilton

Illustrated by Steve Haefele

Based on the Scholastic book series "Clifford The Big Red Dog" by Norman Bridwell

No part of this publication may be reproduced in whole or in part, or stored in a retrieval system, or transmitted in any form or by any means, electronic, mechanical, photocopying, recording, or otherwise, without written permission of the publisher. For information regarding permission, write to Scholastic Inc., Attention: Permissions Department, 557 Broadway, New York, NY 10012.

ISBN 0-439-69045-5

Copyright © 2005 Scholastic Entertainment Inc. All rights reserved. Based on the CLIFFORD THE BIG RED DOG book series published by Scholastic Inc. ™ & © Norman Bridwell. SCHOLASTIC and associated logos are trademarks and/or registered trademarks of Scholastic Inc. CLIFFORD, CLIFFORD THE BIG RED DOG, CLIFFORD'S PUPPY DAYS, and associated logos are trademarks and/or registered trademarks of Norman Bridwell.

10 9 8 7   07 08

Designed by John Daly

Printed in the U.S.A.   First printing, January 2005

SCHOLASTIC INC.

New York   Toronto   London   Auckland   Sydney
Mexico City   New Delhi   Hong Kong   Buenos Aires

In wintertime, Clifford and Emily Elizabeth loved to go sledding.

Clifford and Emily Elizabeth had matching saucer sleds. Clifford's was small and red, just like he was. He called it "Rosebud."

On the day after the first big snowfall, they rode their sleds for hours.

Soon Clifford grew cold from his nose to his toes.

"You're shivering!" said Emily Elizabeth. "It's time to go." She snuggled Clifford into her scarf and they headed home to have hot cocoa.

In their hurry to get home, they forgot Rosebud on the hill.
As the days went by, the snow melted and Rosebud slid farther
down the slope. Soon it was on the sidewalk.

Mr. Sidarsky found it. "I can't believe someone is throwing this out!" he squeaked.

That night, the Sidarskys relaxed in their brand-new heated swimming pool.

Upstairs, Emily Elizabeth was thrilled that it was snowing again.
"We can go sledding tomorrow!" she told Clifford. "Where's your sled?"

Uh-oh, thought Clifford. Where was Rosebud?

Clifford looked everywhere. Rosebud was gone!

He asked his friends.
"I haven't seen a sled anywhere," said Zo.
"Or a rosebud!" said Flo.

"Let's see," said Jorgé. "Is it red?"
"Yes!" answered Clifford.
"Is it round?" asked Jorgé.
"That's it!" shouted Clifford.

"Nope, I haven't seen it," said Jorgé.

"Your sled will turn up," Daffodil promised. "I just know it will. Why don't you ask Norville?"

"I know what happened to your sled!" Norville told Clifford. Clifford smiled and wagged his tail. "What?" he asked. "Someone stole it!" said Norville.

Clifford didn't think anybody would be mean enough to steal his sled.

He headed downstairs to ask the Sidarskys if they had seen it.

"You've had my Rosebud all along?" asked Clifford, laughing. "You mean our swimming pool is your Rosebud?" replied the Sidarskys, giggling.

So Clifford and the Sidarskys made a deal. The mice kept Rosebud whenever Clifford wasn't using it, and Clifford always knew where to find his sled.

Clifford went sledding on Rosebud whenever it snowed . . .
except when he shared the big sled with Emily Elizabeth!